D0764362

Gift of the
Friends of the
Pleasant Hill Library

BILINGÜE/BILINGUAL

Vamos a contar / Counting Books

Playas y bicicletas

Un libro para contar en el verano

Beaches and Bicycles

A Summer Counting Book

por/by Rebecca Fjelland Davis

Consultora de lectura/Reading Consultant:
Jennifer Norford
Consultora Senior/Senior Consultant:
Mid-continent for Research and Education

CAPSTONE PRESS
a capstone imprint

A+ Books are published by Capstone Press,
1710 Roe Crest Drive, North Mankato, Minnesota 56003.
www.capstonepub.com

© 2012 Capstone Press, a Capstone imprint. All rights reserved.
No part of this publication may be reproduced in whole or in part, or stored in a retrieval
system, or transmitted in any form or by any means, electronic, mechanical, photocopying,
recording, or otherwise, without written permission of the publisher.
For information regarding permission, write to Capstone Press,
1710 Roe Crest Drive, North Mankato, Minnesota 56003.

Library of Congress Cataloging-in-Publication Data
Davis, Rebecca Fjelland.
  [Beaches and bicycles. Spanish & English]
  Playas y bicicletas = Beaches and bicycles : un libro para contar en el verano/a summer counting book/
por/by Rebecca Fjelland Davis.
      p. cm.—(Vamos a contar = Counting books)
  Includes index.
  Summary: "A counting book that describes summer related activities and events—in both English
and Spanish"—Provided by publisher.
  ISBN 978-1-4296-8250-3 (library binding)
  1. Counting—Juvenile literature. 2. Summer—Juvenile literature. I. Title. II. Title: Beaches
and bicycles.
  QA113.D37718 2012
  513.2'11—dc23   2011028676

Credits
Jenny Marks, editor; Strictly Spanish, translation services; Ted Williams, designer; Eric Manske,
bilingual book designer; Karon Dubke, photographer; Kelly Garvin, media researcher; Laura Manthe,
production specialist

Photo Credits
Brand X Pictures, 18–19 (all), 23 (large flower, left)
Bruce Coleman Inc./Kim Taylor, 14 (all), 15 (top), 27 (butterflies)
Capstone Press, Karon Dubke, cover (all), 2–3 (all), 6–7, 10–11 (all), 12–13 (all), 16–17 (all), 20–21
    (all), 26 (ice pops, frogs), 28, 29 (all)
Comstock Images, 8–9 (all)
Corbis/Owaki-Kulla, 22–23 (smaller flowers, center), 26–27 (sunflowers); zefa/Laureen Morgane,
    24–25
Photodisc, 15 (bottom), 23 (2 large flowers, right)

Note to Parents, Teachers, and Librarians
Playas y bicicletas/Beaches and Bicycles uses color photographs and a rhyming nonfiction format to
introduce children to various signs of the summer season while building mastery of basic counting skills
in both English and Spanish. It is designed to be read aloud to a pre-reader or to be read independently
by an early reader. The images help early readers and listeners understand the text and concepts
discussed. The book encourages further learning by the following sections: Facts about Summer,
Glossary, Internet Sites, and Index. Early readers may need assistance using these features.

Printed in the United States of America in North Mankato, Minnesota.
012013   007131R

The days are long and school is over.
The fields are full of sweet green clover.
Summer is the season for fun, fun, fun.
Let's count things under summer's sun.

Los días son largos y se terminó la escuela. Los campos están llenos de tréboles verdes. El verano es la estación para divertirse mucho, mucho, mucho. Vamos a contar cosas bajo el sol del verano.

One summer sun is a huge,
bright dot. Warm sun rays
make the days so hot.

Un sol de verano es un punto
gigante y brillante. Los rayos
tibios del sol hacen que los días
sean calurosos.

Two round wheels, come,
let's race! Summertime
moves at such a fast pace.

Dos ruedas redondas, ven,
¡hagamos una carrera!
El verano se mueve a
un ritmo rápido.

3

Three red canoes.
As the days get hotter, take a
lazy trip through cool lake water.

Tres canoas rojas. Cuando los
días se hacen más calurosos,
disfruta un viaje perezoso sobre
el agua fresca del lago.

Four green frogs with big, round eyes look around for a meal of flies.

Cuatro ranas verdes con ojos
grandes y redondos miran
a su alrededor en busca de
una comida de moscas.

11

5

Five round beach balls,
colorful and fun.
Bounce them around
in the summer sun.

12

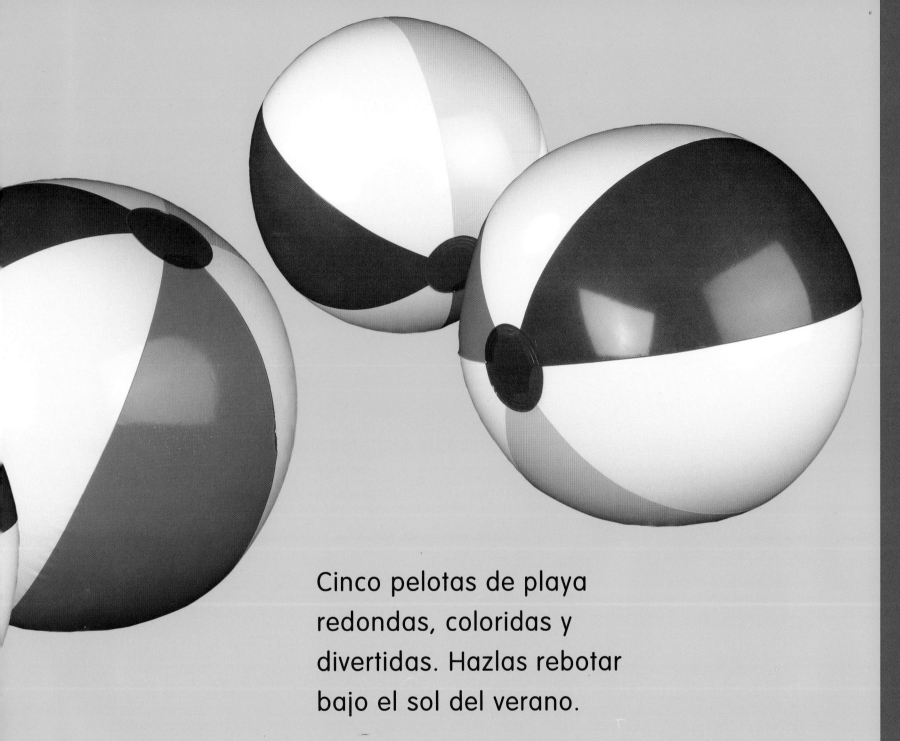

Cinco pelotas de playa
redondas, coloridas y
divertidas. Hazlas rebotar
bajo el sol del verano.

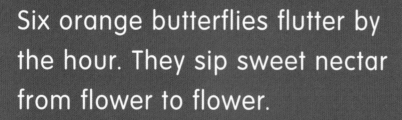

Six orange butterflies flutter by the hour. They sip sweet nectar from flower to flower.

———————————————

Seis mariposas naranjas revolotean alrededor. Ellas beben a sorbos el néctar de flor en flor.

1
2
3
4
5
6
7
8
9
10

Seven fruity ice pops
taste so sweet.
Just what you need
in the summer heat.

Siete helados de jugo
son muy dulces.
Justo lo que necesitas
para el calor del verano.

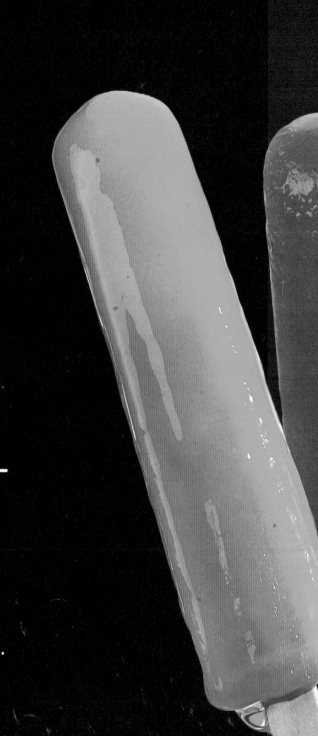

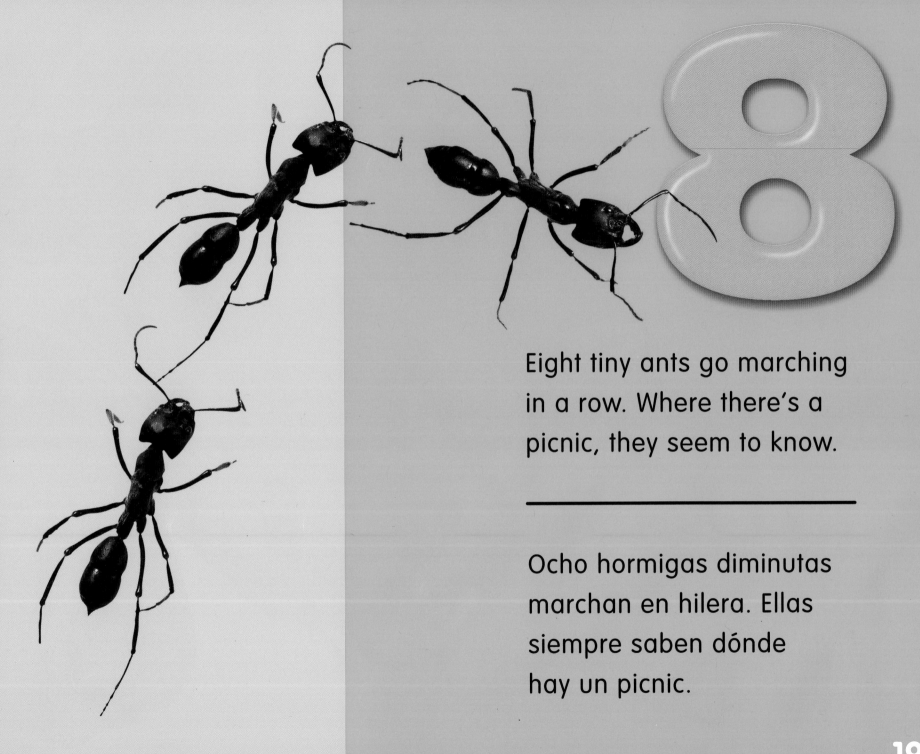

Eight tiny ants go marching
in a row. Where there's a
picnic, they seem to know.

Ocho hormigas diminutas
marchan en hilera. Ellas
siempre saben dónde
hay un picnic.

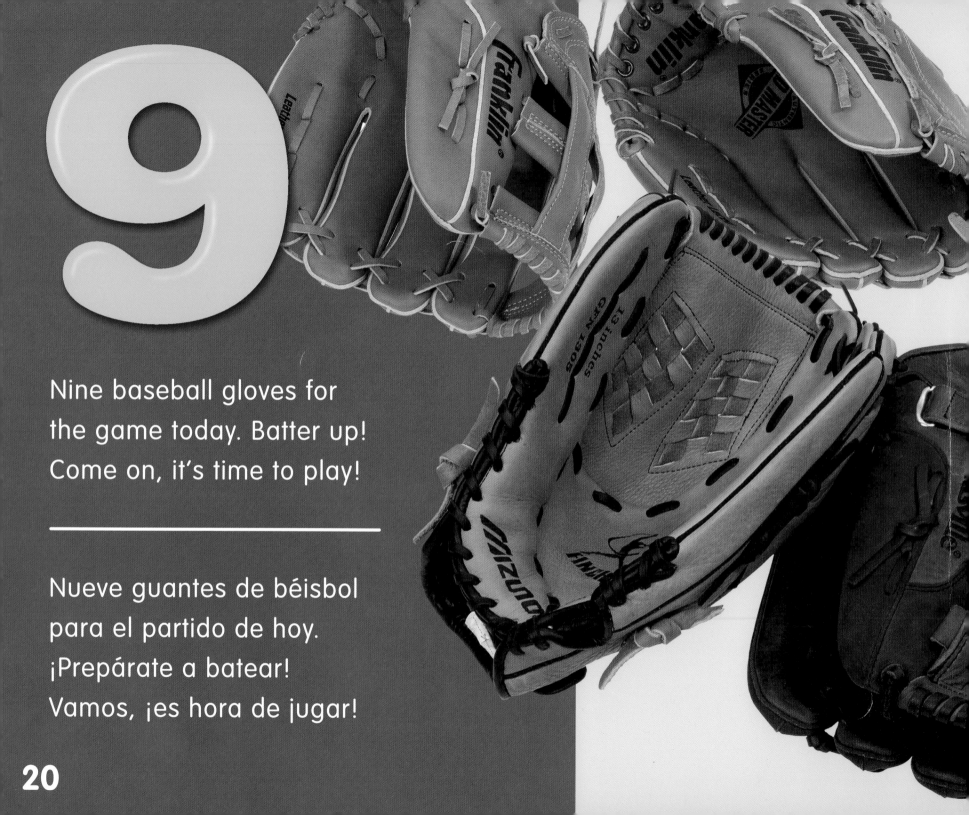

9

Nine baseball gloves for
the game today. Batter up!
Come on, it's time to play!

Nueve guantes de béisbol
para el partido de hoy.
¡Prepárate a batear!
Vamos, ¡es hora de jugar!

Ten yellow sunflowers all face the sun. When their petals start to fade, summer is done.

Diez girasoles amarillos están de cara al sol. Cuando sus pétalos empiezan a decolorarse, se acabó el verano.

10

Summer's days are lazy, long, and hot. So find your way to a cool, wet spot.

————————————

Los días de verano son perezosos, largos y calurosos. Entonces encuentra un lugar fresco y con agua.

How Many?
¿Cuántos hay?

Ice pops /
Helados

Frogs /
Ranas

Butterflies /
Mariposas

Sunflowers /
Girasoles

27

Facts about Summer
Datos del verano

The sun is higher in the sky in the summer than it is in the winter.

El sol está más alto en el cielo en el verano que en el invierno.

When it is summer in North America, it is winter in South America.

Cuando es verano en América del Norte, es invierno en América del Sur.

In summer, the days are longer than the nights. In some places, like northern Alaska, the days are 24 hours long.

En el verano, los días son más largos que las noches. En algunos lugares, como el norte de Alaska, los días duran 24 horas.

**Butterflies drink nectar from flowers.
Bumblebees and hummingbirds do too.**

Las mariposas beben néctar de las flores.
También lo hacen las abejas y los picaflores.

**Butterflies have taste buds on their feet. They step on
flowers to know if the flowers taste good or not.**

Las mariposas tienen papilas gustativas en sus patas.
Ellas pisan las flores para saber si tienen buen o mal sabor.

**There are 20,000 types of ants in the world.
Some ants dig tunnels up to 15 feet long.**

Existen 20,000 tipos de hormigas en el mundo.
Algunas hormigas excavan túneles de hasta
15 pies de largo.

**Sunflowers grow as tall as 15 feet. Some have
flowers 14 inches across.**

Los girasoles pueden crecer hasta 15 pies.
Algunos tienen flores de 14 pulgadas de ancho.

29

Glossary

batter—the player whose turn it is to bat in baseball

flutter—to wave or flap up and down; butterflies flutter their wings

nectar—a sweet liquid in flowers

petal—one of the colored outer parts of a flower

ray—a beam of light

season—one of the four parts of the year; autumn, winter, spring, and summer are seasons

taste bud—a small organ that can tell what things taste like

Internet Sites

FactHound offers a safe, fun way to find Internet sites related to this book. All of the sites on FactHound have been researched by our staff.

Here's all you do:

Visit *www.facthound.com*

Type in this code: 9781429682503

Glosario

el bateador—el jugador que tiene un turno al bate en béisbol

la estación—una de las cuatro partes del año; otoño, invierno, primavera y verano son estaciones

el néctar—un líquido dulce en las flores

las papilas gustativas—un pequeño órgano que puede decir qué gusto tienen las cosas

el pétalo—una de las partes exteriores de la flor

el rayo—un haz de luz

revolotear—volar haciendo giros o vueltas en poco espacio; las mariposas revolotean

Sitios de Internet

FactHound brinda una forma segura y divertida de encontrar sitios de Internet relacionados con este libro. Todos los sitios en FactHound han sido investigados por nuestro personal.

Esto es todo lo que tienes que hacer:

Visita *www.facthound.com*

Ingresa este código: 9781429682503

Index

Índice

Super-cool stuff! Check out projects, games and lots more at www.capstonekids.com

¡Algo súper divertido! Hay proyectos, juegos y mucho más en www.capstonekids.com

3 1901 05790 9931